HEINEMANN Profiles

Margaret Thatcher

Sean Connolly

Heinemann
LIBRARY
SERVICES
CENTRAL ENGLAND

First published in Great Britain by Heinemann
Library, Halley Court, Jordan Hill, Oxford
OX2 8EJ, a division of Reed Educational and
Professional Publishing Ltd.
Heinemann is a registered trademark of Reed
Educational & Professional Publishing Limited.

OXFORD MELBOURNE AUCKLAND
JOHANNESBURG BLANTYRE
GABORONE IBADAN PORTSMOUTH
NH (USA) CHICAGO

© Reed Educational and Professional Publishing
Ltd 2000
The moral right of the proprietor has been
asserted.

Designed by Visual Image
Originated by Dot Gradations
Printed and bound in Hong Kong/China

04 03 02 01 00
10 9 8 7 6 5 4 3 2 1

ISBN 0 431 08630 3

British Library Cataloguing in Publication Data

Connolly, Sean
Margaret Thatcher. – (Heinemann Profiles)
1. Thatcher, Margaret – Juvenile literature
 2. Women prime ministers – Great
 Britain – Biography – Juvenile literature
 3. Prime ministers – Great Britain –
 Biography – Juvenile literature
I. Title
941'.085'092
ISBN 0431086303

Acknowledgements

The Publishers would like to thank the following
for permission to reproduce photographs:
CameraPress: p22; Hulton Getty: pp6, 13, 21, 27;
PA News: pp14, 15, 17, 25, 47, 51; PA Reuter
Photo: p11; Rex Features: pp5, 7, 8, 18, 19, 20,
23, 26, 28, 30, 33, 35, 36, 37, 38, 40, 43, 44, 46,
49, 50; Frank Spooner Pictures: P Piel p31.

Cover photograph reproduced with permission of
Rex Features

Every effort has been made to contact copyright
holders of any material reproduced in this book.
Any omissions will be rectified in subsequent
printings if notice is given to the Publisher.

For more information about Heinemann Library
books, or to order, please phone ++44 (0)1865
888066, or send a fax to ++44 (0)1865 314091.
You can visit our website at
www.heinemann.co.uk.

Any words appearing in the text in bold, **like
this**, are explained in the Glossary.

CONTENTS

WHO IS MARGARET THATCHER?

A young voter turning eighteen years of age in 1990 would have known of only one British prime minister – Margaret Thatcher. She led the country from 1979 until 1990, winning three general elections and shaping British politics in a way that few other leaders have ever done. Apart from being the first woman prime minister in Britain, she held power for a longer period than any other prime minister in the twentieth century.

SOLID VALUES

Margaret Thatcher learned many lessons from her father, Alfred, who taught her the importance of **thrift**, determination and hard work. He also displayed a strong sense of pride in Britain. These were the same values that Mrs Thatcher brought to her Conservative Party as leader, and later to the country as a whole as prime minister. She sought to overturn the decline in the British economy that

'They won't turn the clock back more than a third of the distance. They can't. She's changed the Labour Party far more than the Conservative Party.'

Alan Walters, Conservative adviser, talking about Mrs Thatcher's influence on future Labour Party governments, 1989

Margaret Thatcher's career has been a dramatic example of the 'politics of conviction'.

she had seen in the 1970s, while also pushing strongly for British interests in Europe and beyond.

Few other leaders have given their name to a whole set of values and policies, but people around the world are familiar with the word 'Thatcherism'. Her leadership was consistent and unchanging, so much so that she became known as the 'Iron Lady'.

OPPOSING VOICES

In the end it was her strong opinions that gradually weakened Margaret Thatcher's position as leader, as once-loyal **allies** felt that they no longer had a say in governing the country. Joining with her long-standing **opponents** they delivered the blow that ended her leadership. But even now, she remains a strong presence and her views on British life still find echoes in 'the corridors of power'.

ABOVE THE SHOP

Grantham in the 1920s was a place where hard work and reliability built a person's reputation.

Margaret Thatcher was born Margaret Hilda Roberts in the Lincolnshire town of Grantham on 13 October 1925. Grantham was – and still is – the sort of place that people describe as 'Middle England'. This term usually describes places where people hold traditional values such as honesty, and carefulness with money.

A STRONG INFLUENCE

Margaret's family certainly held these traditional values. Her father, Alfred Roberts, was a successful grocer who had left school at thirteen to set up his own shop. Through hard work and careful planning he had built up his shop into a thriving small business. Both Margaret and her sister, Muriel, were born in a room over the shop. Margaret's mother, Beatrice, was content to stay at home, looking after the two girls and taking care of the housekeeping.

'He [her father] taught me that you first sort out what you believe in. You then apply it. You don't **compromise** on things that matter.'
Margaret Thatcher, 1979

Alfred Roberts was a leader in the local politics of Grantham. He held the post of **alderman** and took his responsibilities seriously. Alfred believed in leading by example and he wanted the voters of Grantham to see that he could offer the town the same virtues that he showed in building up his own business. He was proud of his town and also of being British. Addressing a dinner of Grantham businessmen in 1937 he claimed that he would rather shine shoes in Britain than be 'a leading **citizen** in a good many of the other leading countries in the world today, because I know I can get **tolerance** and justice from my fellow men'.

Alfred Roberts' small corner shop gave Margaret her understanding of the value of money.

Margaret agreed with such statements and would carry the same feelings throughout her own life. She also remembered some other advice he gave his daughters: never hold an opinion simply because other people hold it.

SIMPLE TASTES

The Roberts family belonged to the Methodist Church, which also prizes the sort of hard-working values that Alfred argued for. The family attended church each Sunday and, as a local **councillor**, Alfred tried to ensure that Sundays in Grantham were reserved for worship.

As a schoolgirl, Margaret was always disciplined and neatly turned out.

Alfred extended his belief in simple pleasures and hard work to his family. Even as children, both girls spent hours helping out in the shop, watching as money was carefully counted and lists of expenses were entered into the shop's books. Neither girls had a bicycle and they rarely went to the cinema or the theatre. They were not denied these things because the family was poor: it was simply that Alfred felt that these pleasures were not worth the money they cost. The girls and their mother would rarely have a hot bath as Alfred saved money by not having a hot water system in the house.

SUCCESS AT SCHOOL

Alfred believed in the value of education and was proud when Margaret won a scholarship to Kesteven and Grantham Girls' School, the best school in the area. Margaret was a disciplined child and worked hard at her studies. Her school satchel always bulged with books and she was never shy about asking questions in class. Her school reports showed that she was well behaved and **ambitious**, and several teachers predicted that she would be a great success in later life.

Although Margaret's qualities at school were hard work and discipline, rather than natural brilliance, she did show outstanding qualities in one field – debating. Margaret showed an ability to ask difficult questions and to answer questions she was asked calmly and with great self-confidence. This skill would be very helpful in her later life.

'I don't think she [Margaret] has much of a sense of humour, I don't think her father had and I certainly don't think her mother had.'
Margaret Wickstead, a childhood friend, 1986

THE OUTSIDE WORLD

Kesteven and Grantham Girls' School was proud of the fact that several girls passed the exams each year to enter either Oxford or Cambridge Universities. Margaret was determined to be one of these successful girls, and her father backed her all the way. She had concentrated on chemistry in her last years at school, but she had to revise Latin and other subjects in order to take this important examination. After studying late into the night for several weeks Margaret passed her exams. In 1943 she was offered a place at Somerville College, Oxford, to study chemistry.

AN EXCITING NEW LIFE

Apart from a week spent in London, Margaret had never really been away from Grantham. Oxford was like another world, with its ancient buildings, learned professors and students who came from very rich backgrounds. Most students, unlike Margaret, came from **public schools** and had an easy confidence about everything they did. And also unlike Margaret, they had experience in dealing with people who served them, such as the college **porters** and cleaners.

Margaret, however, retained her common sense and did not let herself get discouraged by her new

Oxford's ancient buildings and centuries-old traditions were a far cry from familiar Grantham.

surroundings. As always, work came first and at an **elite** university such as Oxford, the work was hard. Students who did poor work ran the risk of being expelled. Margaret never ran that risk. Just as she did at school, she let her hard work and discipline overcome her lack of natural brilliance.

UNIVERSITY POLITICS

Margaret became interested in politics as soon as she entered Oxford. Universities are always good places to hear heated political debates, and Margaret soon found herself swept up in them immediately. Her views had been shaped by her father's strong opinions on the importance of careful management of money. These views were echoed by the Conservative Party and Margaret joined the Oxford University Conservative Association (OUCA) in her first term.

The OUCA was largely a social club when Margaret joined, although members sometimes made speeches in the surrounding towns and villages. OUCA members also helped in the war effort, as the Second World War was raging. They collected goods that could be used by the military and helped look after defences in the area.

The 1945 **general election** gave Margaret a taste of national politics. She attended meetings in support of the Conservative **candidate** for Oxford. Margaret also returned to Grantham during the

Party politics

Throughout most of the twentieth century the United Kingdom has been governed by one of two political parties – the Conservative Party or the Labour Party. Each of these parties stands for a set of values and voters choose between the parties – and their overall values – at each election. One major difference between the parties is the way in which they handle government money. The Labour Party has tried to improve conditions of the poor and needy by using **tax** money to help these groups. Tax money also goes to give **unemployed** people an income until they can find another job. The Conservatives, on the other hand, believe that by reducing taxes people will have a chance to keep more of their earnings. With less tax to pay, they argue, people will be encouraged to take risks and set up their own companies. These new companies will in turn create more jobs and help unemployed people in that way.

election, to speak out against a candidate there. Dennis Kendall, the Grantham MP, had first been elected in 1942 and three years later was persuading voters to vote against the Conservatives. Margaret spoke to women's groups in an effort to build support for the Conservatives. Back at Oxford, she led moves to make the OUCA more active and in her last year she was elected president of the organization.

The Independent Grantham M.P., Dennis Kendall. It was, and still is, rare for an independent candidate to be elected without the support of a political party.

PUTTING LEARNING INTO PRACTICE

After receiving her degree in 1945 Margaret knew that she had to put her learning to good use. It was time to stand on her own two feet, as her father might have said. Her first job was doing chemical research for a plastics company in Essex. After working there for four years Margaret found a job testing the quality of cake filings and ice-cream for the Lyons Company in London. Despite her satisfaction with this work, Margaret still had the taste for something else – politics. She had made political connections while working in Essex, so she continued to live there even though her work had moved to London.

FIRST POLITICAL STEPS

Margaret had thoroughly enjoyed her experience with politics while at Oxford and she began to think of ways in which she could build a political career. In 1946 **Parliament** voted in a pay rise for Members of Parliament (MPs), raising their annual salary to £1000 – about £35,000 in today's money. One of the obstacles that Margaret had faced in thinking about politics as a career – the low money earned – evaporated. In her spare time she began studying law, since a good knowledge of the law would be important in politics.

AN EXPECTED SETBACK

Margaret became involved in Conservative associations in Essex and attended the annual Conservative Party Conferences. She set her sights on becoming a **candidate** in the **general election** that was going to take place in 1950. Still only twenty-four years old, she became the Conservative candidate for Dartford, Kent. This **constituency** would almost certainly go to Labour, but the Party officials thought that Margaret would gain from her experience.

Margaret lost the election, as expected, but voters and Conservative officials were impressed with her thoroughness and persistence. The pattern was repeated in the following year's election, and once more Labour held the Dartford seat. But Margaret's political skills and her youth – she was the youngest woman candidate in both elections – ensured that she would not be forgotten.

Newlyweds Denis and Margaret Thatcher were an ideal match for each other.

PARTNER FOR LIFE

Margaret had met a young businessman named Denis Thatcher during her first Dartford **campaign**. The Thatcher family had a successful chemical company in Kent and Denis ran it skilfully. He had been married before the war, but divorced soon afterwards and wanted to marry again. The two admired each other, fell in love and married in December 1951.

The new man in Margaret's life shared many of Alfred Roberts's views. But there was one important difference – unlike Alfred, Denis believed that women should have the chance to explore their chosen careers.

'In this way, gifts and talents that would otherwise be wasted are developed to the benefit of the community.'
Margaret Thatcher, writing about women pursuing careers, 1952

MP FOR FINCHLEY

By marrying someone as wealthy as Denis, Margaret was free to consider politics without any worries about the lack of money she would earn. She was able to leave her job and continue to study law. Margaret passed her bar exams in 1953. That same year she gave birth to twins, Mark and Carol. With the couple's comfortable income, they could afford a live-in nanny, so that Margaret could pursue her goals in the law and politics.

Still, despite the Thatchers' comfortable income, Margaret faced an uphill battle in her early political career. Although Denis supported the idea of female careers, it seemed as though the voters – or at least the Party officials who chose **candidates** – thought otherwise. Of the 625 MPs in the early 1950s, only 17 were women.

AIMING FOR A SEAT

Margaret spent the mid-1950s practising law and looking after her two young children. At the same time she was on the look-out for a **constituency** where she might become the Conservative candidate. She was turned down for several during this time, but in 1958 she was accepted for the north London suburb of Finchley. The choice was ideal – it was close to home as well as to

Parliament itself. Most importantly, it was 'winnable' – at the last election the Conservative candidate had gained a majority of 12,000 votes.

Margaret rose to the challenge, **campaigning** brilliantly and speaking on a wide range of national and international subjects. When the votes were counted in the 1959 election, she had not only won but had increased the majority to 16,260 votes. It was time to enter Parliament.

> 'Should a woman arise equal to the task, I say let her have an equal chance with the men for the leading **Cabinet** posts. Why not a woman **chancellor**? Or **foreign secretary**?'
>
> Margaret Thatcher, 1952

LIFE IN THE COMMONS

The 1959 election was a triumph not only for Margaret Thatcher but for the Conservative Party itself. Under the leadership of Harold Macmillan, the Conservatives returned for their third straight **term** with a **majority** of 100 seats in the **House of Commons**. Macmillan was a popular leader, and British people felt better off with him as Prime Minister. They seemed to echo a comment Macmillan had made in 1957: 'most of our people have never had it so good.'

Britain regained much of its prosperity under the leadership of Prime Minister Harold Macmillan.

GAINING NOTICE

Margaret was **ambitious** and was unlikely to settle for being a **back-bencher**. She showed this from the start. An MP's first **parliamentary** speech is known as their 'maiden speech', and is usually short and a bit dull – simply as a way of getting over 'stage fright'. Margaret, however, spoke without notes for twenty-seven minutes. Fellow Conservatives, and even some Labour MPs, congratulated her on her skilful performance.

Margaret had spoken in favour of a bill to allow the **press** to attend public meetings freely. It was not an earth-shattering bill, but it passed through the Commons and was approved. Margaret showed herself to be well informed about **taxes**. Recognizing a rising star in their ranks, the Conservative parliamentary officials offered her the job of parliamentary secretary at the Ministry of Pensions, which she naturally accepted. Such a posting is usually seen as the first rung in the ladder that climbs to higher offices in government. Margaret's career would prove to be no exception.

THE FRINGES OF POWER

Margaret's new post suited her skills and training – it took someone with great concentration and an eye for detail to read all the documents involved with the job. Margaret performed this role well, even though the posting kept her from the real political action such as major decisions about the economy and foreign affairs.

In the heated political atmosphere of the 1960s, Conservative MP Enoch Powell stirred the passions of many voters. To many, his views were seen as openly racist.

Into Government

I n the end, Margaret's job as parliamentary secretary lasted two years. In 1963 Prime Minister Macmillan resigned because of ill health. Lord Home, who took over as prime minister, narrowly lost the **general election** in 1964 when Harold Wilson led the Labour Party to power with a **majority** of only four.

A developing role

Lord Home was dropped as leader of the Conservative Party after the 1964 defeat and was replaced by Edward Heath. Labour held a slender majority in the Commons, but after the 1966 election increased it to 97. Margaret Thatcher was eager to join the ranks of the party leaders in their attacks on the government.

Her chance came in October 1967 when she was appointed to a minor position within the **Shadow**

Prime Minister Edward Heath (seated, centre) was a powerful political figure who would later become a critic of Mrs Thatcher.

Cabinet. A year later she became Shadow Minister for Education. By now even the most old-fashioned Conservative Party leaders agreed that it was important to have at least one woman in the Shadow Cabinet. No other Conservative woman MP was as experienced as Margaret Thatcher, so her position now seemed secure.

CABINET MEMBER

Prime Minister Harold Wilson called a general election in June 1970. The Labour Party, **opinion polls** and most of the public expected that Wilson would be returned for another **term** as prime minister. The Shadow Cabinet and other senior Conservatives rallied behind their leader in a successful **campaign**, and to everyone's surprise Edward Heath became Prime Minister.

Margaret visited many schools as part of her role as Shadow Minister for Education in the 1960s.

The 1960s had brought about many changes, including the idea that women can and should pursue their own careers. The reasoning that helped Margaret Thatcher enter the Shadow Cabinet – that there should be at least one woman in it – was carried through to the Cabinet itself. Margaret Thatcher became the Secretary of State for Education and Science.

PARTY LEADER

M argaret Thatcher wanted more than a senior government position. Always looking ahead, Margaret felt that she would spend perhaps two years in the post before being moved 'up the ladder' to a more important position.

A STUBBORN LEADER

At first Prime Minister Heath regarded the only female member of his Cabinet very highly. He admired Margaret's ability to get hold of an idea and stay with it. Heath himself had been elected with a promise of making sweeping changes to the country. In Margaret Thatcher he saw a like-minded **ally**.

Gradually, however, things began to change. Heath began to find Margaret's stubbornness tiresome and he came to believe that she would not listen carefully enough before making up her mind. In many ways, Heath's change of view reflected a personal opinion – as if he had begun to form a dislike of her as a person.

Many businesses operated in semi-darkness during a damaging miners' strike in 1973.

ELECTION SETBACK

Even if she had fallen out with the prime minister, Margaret did develop a friendship with another Cabinet member, Keith Joseph. The two were close during the hectic events of 1974. First, in February, the Conservatives lost power in a closely fought **general election**. Heath remained party leader. Meanwhile, Keith Joseph began making public statements about how the Conservatives had lost their way, using his Centre for Policy Studies as a **mouthpiece**.

Keith Joseph's blunder in a public speech opened the door for Mrs Thatcher's bid to be Conservative Party leader.

The Conservatives lost another general election on 10 October 1974 and still Edward Heath refused to resign. Senior Conservatives now aimed for leadership of the party. Joseph announced his intention to be leader but had to abandon his plans when he made an embarrassing speech that seemed to say that poor people should not be allowed to have children. His dropping out meant that Margaret Thatcher was free to try. She announced her plans in early 1975. Like Joseph, she argued that the Conservatives under Heath had not been 'conservative' enough about spending. She also had another powerful ally, the war hero Airey Neave.

CIRCLING FOR THE KILL

Conservative MPs voted in a leadership election on 4 February 1975. In the first ballot Margaret got more votes than Heath, who then resigned. A week later there was a second ballot. This time around, more **candidates** entered, several of whom agreed with Heath's way of leading and had not wanted to run directly against him in the first ballot. The second ballot was decisive: Margaret Thatcher got nearly twice as many votes as her nearest rival, William Whitelaw. She was the new leader.

That vote proved to be a turning point in British politics. It opened up many possibilities for other women, as a woman was now the leader of one of the major political parties. For Margaret Thatcher the next step was, of course, to cap this achievement by becoming prime minister. But first there was the small matter of defeating the Labour government. However, that prospect did not trouble her and she started planning party strategy from the day she took over as leader.

'To me it is like a dream that the next name on the list after Macmillan, Sir Alec Douglas-Home and Edward Heath is Margaret Thatcher.'

Margaret Thatcher, after being elected leader of the Conservative Party, 1975

Mrs Thatcher relished the chance to attack the Labour government during the 1979 election.

LABOUR ISN'T WORKING

Margaret Thatcher's official title became Leader of the **Opposition**. She appointed people to her **Shadow Cabinet**, helped in this job by the two men who had done so much in her leadership **campaign**: Keith Joseph and Airey Neave. Joseph helped her make sure that the Shadow Cabinet was firm about government spending. Neave, more of a political fighter, ensured that Margaret included some tough fighters on her team.

The Labour government at the time was led by James Callaghan. By 1978 Labour policies were beginning to look badly planned, and during the winter of 1978–9 many public-sector employees went on **strike**. The newspapers referred to this period as the 'winter of discontent', echoing a phrase from the Shakespeare play *Richard III*. For the Conservatives, however, the disruption was good news. They attacked Labour for being a weak government and also for making people lose their jobs. A general election was called for May 1979. The Conservatives were ready with their campaign slogan – 'Labour isn't working'.

PRIME-MINISTER THATCHER

The Labour government of James Callaghan was weak in several ways. In addition to the **strikes** and **trade union** disputes, people worried about the British **currency**. Margaret Thatcher and her Conservative team attacked on all these fronts, pouring scorn on the government, both in **Parliament** and in **campaign** speeches to voters.

A number of strikes in early 1979 weakened the Labour government on the eve of the election.

ACHIEVING A GOAL

The Conservatives began to spell out how things would be different if they won the next **general election** and Margaret Thatcher became prime minister. They promised strong and decisive government, with firm action taken to control unions and to keep government spending – and

'The question you will have to consider is whether we risk tearing everything up by the roots.'
  Prime Minister James Callaghan, referring to Conservative plans in the 1979 election

taxes – as low as possible. They also hinted at one of the policies that would become so closely linked to the name of Margaret Thatcher – **privatization**. The Conservatives intended to sell the National Freight Corporation, which at the time was owned by the **state**, to the public.

The combination of Margaret Thatcher's style, the poor performance of Labour, and Conservative election statements proved to be decisive. On the night of 3 May 1979, as general election votes were counted in each **constituency**, it became clear that Labour was losing ground. The final count showed that the Conservatives would be forming the new government, with a majority of 43 in the **House of Commons**. And leading the party – and the government – would be Britain's first woman prime minister, Margaret Thatcher.

A jubilant Magaret Thatcher, with husband Denis by her side, acknowledged the cheers after her 1979 election victory.

Soldiers landing on the Falkland Islands in the South Atlantic.

THE 'IRON LADY'

The Conservatives had been swept to power largely because voters felt that Labour was weak in its handling of the British economy. The Conservatives promised firmer leadership in this area. But Margaret Thatcher was going to show that she could be equally forceful in international matters. The late 1970s was still the era of the **Cold War**, and Mrs Thatcher believed that the UK, along with its **allies** in **NATO** such as the United States, should stand firm against the **Soviet Union** and its allies.

Mrs Thatcher's stance had earned her the nickname the 'Iron Lady' even before she was prime minister – now it was used more often. She showed her strength when Iranian **terrorists** held nineteen people **hostage** in the Iranian Embassy in London. Mrs Thatcher ordered a Special Air Service (SAS) team to storm the embassy. After a dramatic battle – during which four of the five gunmen were killed – the SAS rescued all the hostages.

THE FALKLANDS CAMPAIGN

Another international event dominated Mrs Thatcher's first **term** – the Falklands conflict. The Falkland Islands are British lands lying in the South Atlantic Ocean, near the southern tip of South America. For many years Argentina had claimed that the islands were theirs, and on 2 April 1982 they invaded and captured the islands. The action was immediately **condemned**, not just by Britain but by the **United Nations**.

Mrs Thatcher reacted swiftly and with great determination. Within three days a huge **task force** set off on the 8000-mile journey to recapture the islands and to reclaim British **sovereignty**. The United States, led by President Ronald Reagan – an admirer of Mrs Thatcher – tried in vain to use **diplomacy** to avoid an all-out war.

After several naval clashes near the islands, the British forces landed on the Falklands on 21 May. After two weeks of heavy fighting they made their way to the capital, Port Stanley, where they finally overcame the Argentine forces. Argentina surrendered on 14 June. The world saw this as a victory not only for Britain, but for Mrs Thatcher herself.

'Failure? The possibility does not exist.'
Margaret Thatcher, referring to the Falklands campaign, April 1982

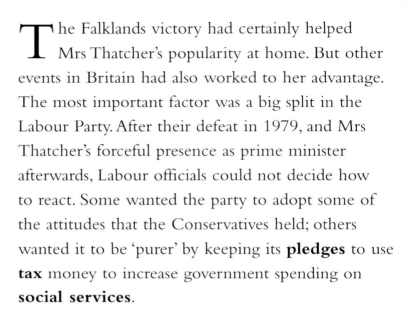

A SECOND TRIUMPH

The Falklands victory had certainly helped Mrs Thatcher's popularity at home. But other events in Britain had also worked to her advantage. The most important factor was a big split in the Labour Party. After their defeat in 1979, and Mrs Thatcher's forceful presence as prime minister afterwards, Labour officials could not decide how to react. Some wanted the party to adopt some of the attitudes that the Conservatives held; others wanted it to be 'purer' by keeping its **pledges** to use **tax** money to increase government spending on **social services**.

Labour leader Michael Foot was well respected, but unable to control some members of the Labour Party or to defeat Mrs Thatcher.

DIVIDED OPPOSITION

In 1980 the Labour Party chose Michael Foot to replace James Callaghan as leader. Foot was a respected politician who came from the 'purer' wing of the party. Mrs Thatcher was pleased with this news since she felt that Foot represented outdated opinions that were out-of-touch with the voters. Others, including many in the Labour Party agreed. In 1981 four leading Labour MPs – Roy Jenkins, Shirley Williams, David Owen and William Rodgers – left the Labour Party to form a new party. The new Social Democratic Party then formed an alliance with the Liberal Party, which had been a weak party since the end of the First World War. Their aim was to break the two-party system of either Labour or Conservative. However, their immediate effect was to divide those who opposed Mrs Thatcher's Conservative Party.

THE 'FALKLANDS FACTOR'

Mrs Thatcher was satisfied with the British political scene after all of these events. She called for a **general election** to be held on 9 June 1983. The **Opposition**, now divided, spent much of their time arguing among themselves and offering confused messages to voters. Mrs Thatcher, on the other hand, presented herself as a strong leader and very much the 'Iron Lady'. Her success in the Falklands played a huge part in the election – this advantage was known as the 'Falklands Factor'.

Mrs Thatcher sat in a tank in 1983 during a triumphant visit to the Falklands after their recapture.

The Conservatives won the election in the largest **landslide** since Labour's victory in 1945. Their majority was increased to a huge 144, which meant that nearly every **bill** recommended by Mrs Thatcher and her team would become law.

TAKING ON THE MINERS

The morning of 10 June 1983 was 'business as usual' for Mrs Thatcher as she looked ahead to a new **term** of office. With such a weak opposition in **Parliament** she knew that many of the plans that had simply been ideas in her first term could now be put into action. Chief among these was a way of controlling the power of **trade unions**.

Most people agreed that the unions had become too powerful. With their power to **strike** they could cripple the country and weaken the government. Edward Heath's defeat in 1974 had been caused largely by a strike in the mining industry. Mrs Thatcher wanted new laws that would limit the power of unions to call strikes. She also knew that the biggest **opponent** to these laws would be the powerful National Union of Miners (NUM), led by Arthur Scargill.

The coal industry was run by a government-owned company known as the National Coal Board. Under Mrs Thatcher's advice the company began to close

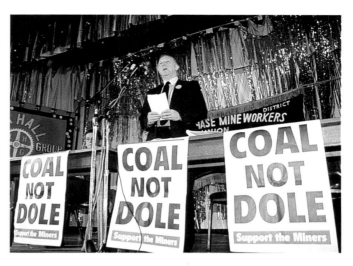

Miners' leader Arthur Scargill defied Mrs Thatcher during the bitter miners' strike that started in 1984. Mrs Thatcher's battle with the NUM had a devastating effect on many communities in Britain's coal-mining areas.

mines that were not producing enough coal. The union's reaction was swift and fierce. In March 1984 Arthur Scargill called a national miners' strike. This action soon turned violent, as striking miners attacked those who crossed **picket lines**. Thousands of police officers were moved around the country to control the violence. At one point Arthur Scargill was arrested for promoting violence.

Throughout the long strike, miners lost money and families were divided as some members went back to work. To Mrs Thatcher, Arthur Scargill had been the symbol of everything she opposed. She was tremendously pleased when the NUM finally voted to end the strike on 3 March 1985.

'We had to fight an enemy without in the Falklands. We always have to be aware of the enemy within, which is more difficult to fight and more dangerous to liberty.'
Mrs Thatcher, during the miners' strike, 1984

ESCAPE FROM DEATH

Mrs Thatcher and the rest of the country knew that the miners would eventually lose their battle with the government. By mid–1984 many miners were already returning to work. By the time the Conservatives were to stage their annual conference in October, Mrs Thatcher sensed the victory lay ahead. Nevertheless, the mood in the country was tense. Mrs Thatcher accused the new Labour leader, Neil Kinnock, of aiding the NUM in its strike and allying itself to the 'wreckers against the workers'.

A TERRIBLE SHOCK

It was in this fighting mood that Mrs Thatcher arrived in Brighton for the Conservative Conference. Then something terrible and unexpected happened. A bomb exploded in the Grand Hotel, where Mrs Thatcher and many senior Conservatives were staying. Mrs Thatcher escaped without injury but five people were killed, and two of her leading Cabinet members, Norman Tebbit and John Wakeham, were injured.

The bomb had been planted by the **Irish Republican Army** (IRA) and Mrs Thatcher had been its intended

> This was a day I wasn't meant to see.'
> Mrs Thatcher, observing a fine autumn day after the Brighton bombing

victim. Television viewers around the world saw the horrific images of the dead and wounded being removed from the rubble. In the middle of it all Mrs Thatcher walked steadily towards the assembled TV cameras. Showing no signs of fright, she said calmly 'It was an attempt not only to disrupt and **terminate** our conference. It was an attempt to cripple Her Majesty's **democratically** elected government.'

RENEWED DETERMINATION

Mrs Thatcher's personal experience of **terrorist** violence strengthened her resolve to set an example for other terrorist organizations around the world. Notably, she refused to meet members of the African National Congress (ANC) of South Africa. The ANC leader, Nelson Mandela, had been imprisoned since 1964 for leading the struggle against the unfair **apartheid** laws in his country. In Mrs Thatcher's view, however, giving support to the pleas for his release would be like helping the IRA in her own country.

The IRA bomb destroyed a large portion of the Grand Hotel in Brighton in 1984.

THE NEW ECONOMY

Mrs Thatcher's defeat of the miners had been the largest of several battles with **trade unions** during her first **terms** as prime minister. The disputes themselves arose in large part because of the **legislation** that the Conservatives had put in place. The most important piece of legislation was the Employment Act, 1982. This called for many limits to be placed on unions. In particular it attacked the notion of the 'closed shop', whereby all the workers in a particular company had to be members of a certain union. The Employment Act protected those who suffered because of the closed-shop system, but it also gave employers greater freedom to sack workers who took part in a strike. The right to strike itself was also limited, and union members had to vote for strike action before it could take place.

Many people applied to buy shares in British Telecom (BT) when it was privatized.

THATCHERISM

Labour law, as this union legislation was called, was only one part of the economic strategy planned by Mrs Thatcher's government. She had always felt that people should be able to stand on their own two feet without government interference. She also believed that the public would become more **prosperous** if more people owned **shares** in companies.

Lord King, a political ally of Mrs Thatcher, became chairman of British Airways after the company was privatized in 1987.

Added to this wish for increased share ownership was Mrs Thatcher's belief that the government should not continue to control the large companies that provided services for the whole country (such as telephone, energy and travel). If these companies had to compete with other companies instead of relying on 'hand-outs' of government money, they were expected to become more efficient and successful.

The Conservatives combined these two aims in a process known as **privatization**. Government-owned companies were sold to private buyers, and the public could buy shares in them. Huge government companies such as British Telecom, British Gas and British Airways were sold off in this way. Privatization, coupled with the tough labour legislation, became known as 'Thatcherism'.

A THIRD VICTORY

PRIME MINISTER   BERNARD INGHAM

The blunt and no-nonsense Bernard Ingham was an ideal press secretary for Mrs Thatcher.

In December 1984 Mrs Thatcher invited a dynamic **Soviet** politician named Mikhail Gorbachev to Britain. Although this was still the era of the **Cold War** she sensed that he was a new type of Soviet official, one who might be more prepared to listen to opposing views and to **compromise**. Gorbachev was impressed by what he saw in Britain – **prosperous** country villages, supermarkets full of things to buy and highly respected scientific centres. It was obvious to Gorbachev that his own country could not match these elements of British life, and he was prepared to say so. He also seemed ready to listen to other people's opinions – something else that set him apart from other Soviet politicians.

INTERNATIONAL GO-BETWEEN

The Gorbachev visit proved to be extremely important for Mrs Thatcher. Within three months of the visit, Gorbachev had become leader of the Soviet Union. He had formed a bond that bordered on friendship with Mrs Thatcher and sent her a warm-hearted message on her sixtieth birthday in October 1985. Mrs Thatcher was also friendly with Ronald Reagan, leader of the other **superpower**, the United States. Reagan was a popular president, but he lacked the searching intelligence that Gorbachev had shown on his British visit. To President Reagan, any Soviet leader would be impossible to understand. Mrs Thatcher, on the other hand, found herself able to deal with both leaders and sometimes paved the way for better understanding between them.

THE COUNTRY DECIDES

No matter how successful a political leader is in managing international matters, the public usually judges them on how the government has affected their daily life. In this area – the economy – Mrs Thatcher felt confident. **Inflation**, which had been a severe problem in the 1970s, was under control. Average earnings, or the amount people bring home to their families, had continued to rise since

'I like Mr Gorbachev; I can do business with him.'
Mrs Thatcher, at the end of Gorbachev's 1984 visit to Britain

the 1983 election. Most importantly, the government was on its way to keeping its promise of reducing the amount of **taxes** that individuals paid to the government.

By 1986 everyone knew that there would be another election soon, probably in mid-1987. Both sides were confident about victory. The Conservatives had their economic achievements, and in particular Mrs Thatcher's image as a strong leader at home and in international matters. The **Opposition** – both the Labour Party and the SDP-Liberal Alliance – felt that continued unemployment and arguments about spending within the Conservative Party itself would help them. Labour felt that its leader, Neil Kinnock, would appeal to the young.

Rupert Murdoch, owner of many newspapers, provided loyal support for Mrs Thatcher's election campaigns.

In the end, the election came in June 1987. The **campaign** had been bitter all along, but the final vote showed that Mrs Thatcher had held the day. The Conservatives were returned with a **majority** of 102 – proof that the country agreed with Thatcherism, or perhaps that it was still worried about Labour.

A rare defeat

In December 1984 the ruling body of Oxford University decided to award an **honorary degree** to Mrs Thatcher. Many people felt that there was nothing unusual about this idea, since several of the previous prime ministers – including Macmillan, Heath and Wilson – had been awarded similar degrees. However, many teachers at the university protested. They argued that Mrs Thatcher and her government had done very little to help education in Britain. Those who were against the degree argued that the government had not given enough money to all forms of learning – from primary schools to scientists who needed money to continue their research. Many leading scientists, they said, had to leave the country to continue their research. Mrs Thatcher's supporters were disgusted by the protests, and even more disgusted in January 1985, when the Oxford teachers voted 738 to 319 not to award the degree. It was Mrs Thatcher's first defeat since she lost the Dartford vote in the 1951 **general election**. She reacted with dignity but felt hurt, and the experience left her more eager to prove the protesters wrong by winning another general election.

Storm Clouds

There is no doubt that the 1987 victory was a triumph for Mrs Thatcher and her Conservative government. Their **majority** had been reduced but remained high enough to push laws easily through **Parliament**. But despite the sense of joy and relief among Conservatives, there were signs of unease. One of these signs came from the very fact that they had won yet another election. Some Conservatives felt that life had become too easy for their party and that an occasional defeat would cause them to look at new ideas. Others, like former-Prime-Minister Heath, seemed to hold a personal grudge against Mrs Thatcher and her unwavering attitudes. Conservatives who felt that 'Thatcherism' relied too heavily on cutting costs were called 'wets'; now their voices were added to the internal debate.

> 'Europe will be stronger precisely because it has France as France, Spain as Spain, Britain as Britain, each with its own customs, traditions and identity. It would be **folly** to try to fit them into some sort of identikit European personality.'
>
> Mrs Thatcher, part of her famous 'Bruges speech', 1988

Dealing with Europe

Nowhere were the disputes within the Conservative Party more public than on the subject of Europe. Many of the Conservative 'wets', along with similar-minded **Opposition** members, felt that Mrs Thatcher did not present a good image of Britain within Europe as a

whole. As a leading member of the **European Community** (EC), Britain was expected to play a role in lessening the difference between European countries. By reducing these differences the EC could play a larger part in building trade within Europe.

Mrs Thatcher, on the other hand, seemed to have an 'us against them' attitude towards Europe. She fought hard to protect Britain's interests, sometimes being the only European leader to **veto** EC proposals. Although some British people believed that her efforts to reduce the amount that Britain had to pay to the EC was a valuable aim, others felt that she was too negative. Mrs Thatcher opposed every effort to build a **federal** Europe since she felt it would weaken Britain's **sovereignty**. She spelled out her views most clearly in a speech she made in the Belgian city of Bruges in September 1988.

Removed from Office

The whole issue of Europe – and the divisions that it would cause within the Conservative Party – became quite complicated. One area in particular attracted public attention, and a good deal of criticism of the way the Conservatives approached the problem. This area involved two elements that Mrs Thatcher felt strongly about – money and British **sovereignty**.

The problem came to a head in 1989 with the discussion about what was known as the Exchange Rate Mechanism (ERM). The ERM was a system designed to tie European **currencies** together so that no single currency would become too strong or weak. Many senior Conservatives, including the **Chancellor of the Exchequer** Nigel Lawson, believed that Britain would gain by entering the ERM. Mrs Thatcher, however, resisted any moves to

Violent demonstrations, even in some Conservative strongholds, typified the public's angry response to the Poll Tax.

limit Britain's freedom to control its own currency, the pound sterling. Eventually, on 26 October 1989, Nigel Lawson resigned from office.

THE POLL TAX

At around the same time there was an equally difficult problem at home – and again it had to do with money. It centred on a type of local **tax** officially called the community charge but informally known as the 'poll tax'. For years many Conservatives had felt that the rates' system – the system of taxes used to pay for local services – was unfair. Under this system, people paid local taxes according to the value of their house. Someone living in an expensive house would pay much more than the owner of a small flat. **Tenants** would not even pay any rates. This seemed unfair because all of these people enjoyed the same services such as rubbish collection, street repairs and so on.

The Conservatives had thought of a new style of taxation, which they included in the 1987 election **manifesto**. Called the community charge, the system would impose exactly the same local tax on each adult individual. At first this seemed to promise a fairer system. Soon after the election, however, complaints grew. Many people reacted angrily at the idea of a system that would let the very rich pay no more than the very poor.

A BAD COMBINATION

Poll **tax** protests increased in the years after the 1987 election. The Conservatives planned to introduce it in Scotland first, and then in the rest of the UK. Many Conservatives began to worry about the angry reaction, and they tried to distance themselves from the policy. Michael Heseltine, who had held **Cabinet** positions in the first Thatcher governments, was one of the most forceful critics of the poll tax.

By 1990 the Conservatives had begun to look weak and divided on both the poll tax and the issues surrounding the ERM and Europe in general. The new tax was introduced in England and Wales in April 1990 and the Conservatives lost many votes in local elections held in May. The poll tax protests reached dramatic heights, with riots and disruptions in London and elsewhere. Behind the scenes Heseltine was meeting many Conservative MPs, and it was an open secret that he was waiting for a chance to take Mrs Thatcher's place as party leader and prime minister.

Geoffrey Howe's dramatic resignation speech in November 1990 signalled the beginning of the end of Mrs Thatcher's position as Prime Minister.

THE FINAL BLOW

Geoffrey Howe had been **Foreign Secretary** for many years but his views on Europe had differed from Mrs Thatcher's. She removed him from that position in July 1989 but kept him in the Cabinet. Howe was insulted by this and came to believe that Mrs Thatcher had long since lost the ability to listen to people. On 13 November 1990 he resigned from the Cabinet by making a dramatic speech in **Parliament**. With such divisions opening up at the highest levels, the Conservative Party decided on a leadership vote among its MPs. This vote would either confirm Mrs Thatcher as leader – and Prime Minister – or it would replace her with a new leader.

Within days an election was held among Conservative MPs. Heseltine declared himself a **candidate**. In the first round of voting Mrs Thatcher received more votes than Heseltine but not enough to avoid a second round. But the result really showed that MPs had lost confidence overall and Mrs Thatcher knew that she should step down. She made her final speech as Prime Minister on 22 November 1990 and resigned on 28 November.

Denis, loyal as ever, watched as Mrs Thatcher stepped down from office on 28 November 1990.

LADY THATCHER

Mrs Thatcher had waited six days before stepping down as Prime Minister so that the party could elect a new leader in that time. She drew some relief from the fact that her favourite to succeed her, John Major, won the vote on 27 November. Major became the new Conservative leader and Prime Minister when Mrs Thatcher resigned.

AMONG THE LORDS

As Prime Minister, one of John Major's first acts was to **ennoble** Mrs Thatcher. She became Lady Thatcher of Kesteven in June 1991. With this new title she left the **House of Commons** to begin her new role in the **House of Lords**, the upper house of **Parliament**. Lady Thatcher often attends sessions of the House of Lords, and her speeches still draw the attention of journalists and the public. She is still able to communicate her views on British life and on international matters.

'I waved and got into the car with Denis beside me, as he always has been; and the car took us past **press**, policemen and the tall black gates of Downing Street ... out to whatever the future held.'
Mrs Thatcher, describing her departure as prime minister, in *The Downing Street Years*

FOREIGN POPULARITY

Mrs Thatcher enjoyed a good relationship with US President Reagan and with Americans in general. Since her resignation she has been invited by many groups – especially in the United States – to make speeches or to accept awards.

BROADER INTERESTS

Being removed from the hustle and bustle of daily political life has allowed Lady Thatcher to pursue other interests. In 1993 she published her political **memoirs**, which provided a fascinating glimpse at life behind the scenes during her leadership. Lady Thatcher has also had more time to devote to travel and to her family, including her grandchildren. And her husband Denis, who had been the butt of much good-natured teasing while Mrs Thatcher was Prime Minister, is free to play more of his beloved golf in the company of family friends.

Although leader of the Labour Party, Prime Minister Tony Blair recognizes many of Mrs Thatcher's accomplishments.

Margaret Thatcher is the type of leader who inspires strong feelings. The values that she represented, especially her strong sense of national pride and the steadfast pursuit of the economic policies now known as 'Thatcherism', are ones people tend to heartily agree with or disagree with. But, whatever their views, many people respect the woman whose name is so linked with them.

INTERNATIONAL APPEAL

There is an interesting parallel between Margaret Thatcher and Mikhail Gorbachev, the **Soviet** leader she so respected in the late 1980s. Both have long since lost their powerful political roles, but nonetheless remain widely respected away from their own countries. Foreigners see only the obvious benefits of what these leaders achieved – such as material wealth for some people. Many within their countries, however, believe that this wealth has come at a terrible cost and they are still paying for the social divisions produced by these leaders.

BRITISH ACKNOWLEDGEMENT

Many observers have noticed the Thatcher influence on the Labour government of Tony Blair, even though the Labour Party fought so hard against 'Thatcherism'. Blair's tough position during the Kosovo crisis in 1999, coupled with his government's urging that people be encouraged to stand up on their own two feet, can be traced directly to Mrs Thatcher. Blair himself is unashamed to admit how much he respects the former Prime Minister.

As Baroness Thatcher, Margaret Thatcher sits in the House of Lords. She is shown here in her ceremonial robes for the state opening of Parliament.

Even more curiously, the divisions in the Conservative Party that led to Mrs Thatcher's downfall were not resolved after her departure. Although the poll tax was long gone, the split over Europe remained, waiting to erupt at any time and possibly to split the party.

'Like Winston Churchill, she is known for her courage, conviction, determination and willpower. Like Churchill she thrives on **adversity**.'
> Inscription on the Winston Churchill Foundation Award, presented to Mrs Thatcher in Washington, 1988

MARGARET THATCHER– TIMELINE

1925	Margaret Hilda Roberts born in Grantham, Lincolnshire
1936	Enrols at Kesteven and Grantham Girls School
1943	Enters Somerville College, Oxford University
1943	Joins Oxford University Conservative Association (OUCA)
1946	Becomes president of the OUCA
1946	Graduates from Oxford University and takes a job as a research chemist
1950	Loses in election to become MP for the Dartford, Kent, constituency
1951	Loses in second attempt to become MP for Dartford
1951	Marries Denis Thatcher
1953	Gives birth to twins – Mark and Carol
1953	Passes bar exams and begins practising as a lawyer
1959	Elected MP for Finchley, north London
1961	Appointed parliamentary secretary at the Ministry of Pensions
1967	Becomes member of the Shadow Cabinet, responsible for power
1969	Becomes Shadow Minister for Education
1970	Becomes member of the Cabinet (responsible for education) when the Conservatives gain power
1975	Becomes leader of the Conservative Party, succeeding Edward Heath
1979	Leads Conservative Party to victory in general election, becoming prime minister
1982	Leads Britain to victory in Falklands conflict with Argentina
1983	Wins second general election

1984	Survives IRA bomb attack at Grand Hotel, Brighton
1985	Defeats Arthur Scargill's strike of mine workers
1987	Wins third general election
1988	Makes famous 'Bruges speech' about Britain's role in Europe
1990	Stands down as party leader and prime minister after Conservative MPs vote in leadership contest
1991	Becomes Lady Thatcher of Kesteven and takes seat in the House of Lords

GLOSSARY

adversity terrible hardship

alderman a member of the ruling group of a local council

ally a person or country that acts as a partner in case of a dispute

ambitious eager to succeed

apartheid a former system of South African laws that made it hard for black people to live freely

back–bencher an MP who does not hold a post in either the Cabinet or Shadow Cabinet

bar exams the exams that barristers must pass in order to practise law

bill an item debated in Parliament, which if passed becomes law

cabinet a group of MPs chosen by the prime minister to deal with specific areas of ruling the country

campaign a series of planned events to help win an election

candidate someone who stands for office at an election

chancellor of the exchequer the Cabinet member responsible for running the economy

citizen a person who has full legal rights in a country

Cold War the period from 1945 to 1990 when the United States and its allies were prepared to fight the Soviet Union and its allies

compromise when two groups or individuals solve a problem so that each side gives in a little

condemn to criticize harshly

constituency the area that an MP represents in Parliament

councillor in Britain, a person who is elected to a council

currency the name of the unit of money that a country uses

democratically by means of democracy – the political system that gives all adults the right to vote

diplomacy solving of problems by discussion rather than by warfare

elite a small group of people who have an advantage such as more money or intelligence over the general public

employer an individual or organization that employs (uses the labour of) other people

ennoble to give a special title

European Community (EC) former name of the European Union, a group of European countries with economic and political ties

federal central body, but allowing areas to keep certain powers

folly a terrible mistake

foreign secretary the head of the government department dealing with international matters

general election an election in which the whole country votes for MPs, and who will govern in the next session of Parliament

honorary degree a degree which recognizes the value of a particular person

hostage a person held against their will, usually under threat of death

House of Commons the 'lower' house of the British Parliament, where new bills are first debated before becoming law

House of Lords the 'upper' house of the British Parliament, where bills are finally debated before becoming law

inflation a condition of the economy, when prices – and usually wages – keep rising very quickly

Irish Republican Army (IRA) an illegal organization that aims to reunite Northen Ireland with the Irish Republic, and which has used terrorism to try to achieve its aim

landslide an overwhelming victory

legislation another name for the process of law-making in Parliament

majority the amount of votes by which a candidate is elected, or the number of extra seats the governing political party has in Parliament

manifesto a plan of action promised by a political party

memoirs notes, diaries and recollections

mouthpiece a person or group that states the opinions of someone else

NATO the North Atlantic Treaty Organization, a military group formed to represent the United States and its allies in the Cold War

opinion polls the results of series of questions put to the public

opponent a person who argues against another

Opposition the political party or parties that do not form the government, and which usually oppose government legislation

Parliament law-making body

picket line line of people supporting those workers who are on **strike**

pledge a promise, as in an election

policy a system of political plans

porter someone who carries packages

press journalists generally

privatization the selling of companies or property owned by the government to private individuals or companies

prosperous comfortably well off

public school in Britain, a private school

Shadow Cabinet a group of Opposition MPs who are ready to become the next Cabinet if the government is voted out.

shares part-ownership in companies which the public can buy

social services government-run services for needy people

sovereignty the accepted right to govern an area or a country

Soviet relating to the Soviet Union

Soviet Union the former name of Russia and some of its neighbours

state the government, as opposed to individuals

strike stop work in order to force an employer to give in on disputed issues

superpower each of the two main countries, the United States and the Soviet Union, during the Cold War

task force military weapons and troops sent abroad

taxes the money that a government receives from its citizens

tenant someone who pays rent to live in a house or flat

term period someone is elected for

terminate to end completely

terrorist someone who uses illegal violence for a political purpose

thrift care with money

tolerance patient understanding

trade union a group of people who unite to improve working conditions

unemployed without work and unable to find another job

United Nations where representatives of all countries discuss world affairs

veto to vote against something

INDEX

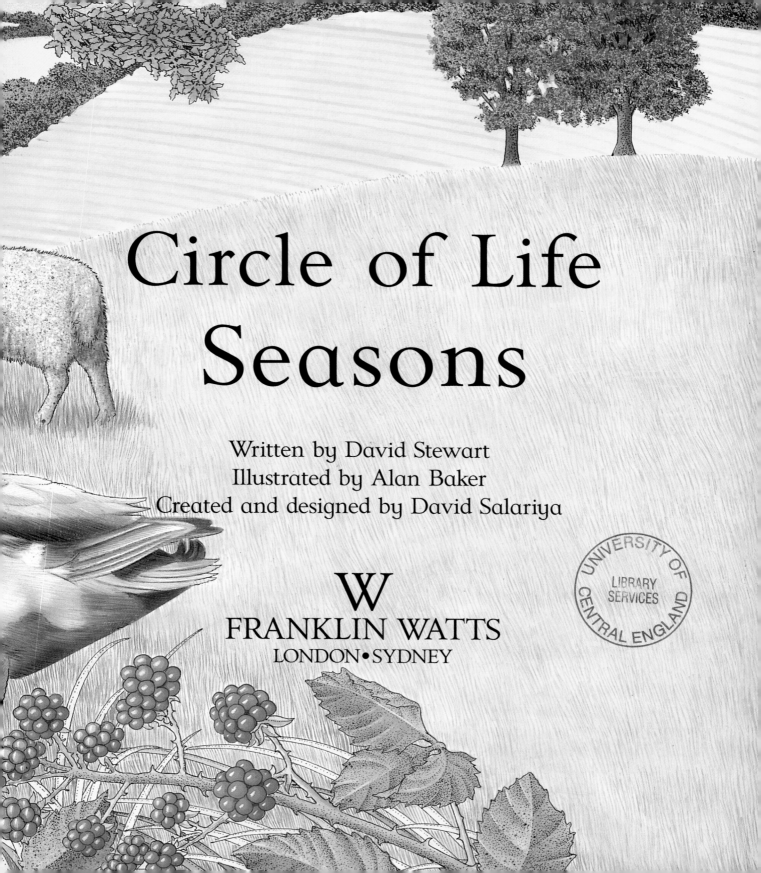

Circle of Life
Seasons

Written by David Stewart
Illustrated by Alan Baker
Created and designed by David Salariya

W
FRANKLIN WATTS
LONDON • SYDNEY

Contents

Introduction

The earth travels around the sun.
It takes one year for the earth to
travel all the way round the sun.

The earth leans at an angle as it travels so one half of
it is closer to the sun. That makes the seasons change:
from spring to summer, summer to autumn,
autumn to winter, and winter back to spring.

When the northern half of the earth is
leaning closer to the sun, it becomes warmer.
This is summer. While this is happening in the north,
it is winter in the southern half of the earth.

Six months later, the northern half of the earth
is leaning away from the sun
and becomes colder.
It is now winter in the north
and summer in the south.

N

Northern half of
the earth

Southern
half of
the earth

7

A tree in spring

After the long cold winter the weather in spring starts to get warmer.

The warmth from the sun makes the buds on the oak tree grow into tiny, bright green leaves.

Squirrels and birds build nests in the branches of the tree. Insects such as moths and beetles feed on the tree, eating leaves and wood.

A tree in summer

By summer the young,
bright green leaves have
grown into strong,
dark green leaves.

Through the summer
acorns are growing at the
tip of the branches.

Down among the roots of
the tree, rabbits are living
in burrows.

9

A tree in autumn

In autumn, as the
weather gets cooler,
the leaves on the oak tree
begin to turn brown.
They fall to the ground.

The acorns also fall
to the ground.

Acorns do not stay on the
ground long: lots of birds and
mammals like to eat them.

A tree in winter

As winter comes,
it gets colder.

All the leaves fall
from the tree, leaving
its branches bare apart
from tiny buds.

Even in the cold of winter, the
buds on the tree contain tiny
leaves, waiting to grow when the
weather gets warmer.

Early spring

In spring, the weather starts to get warmer.

Plants and trees begin to grow.

Baby animals are born in the spring. They will have the warm summer in which to grow strong.

Ewe

This ewe is feeding her newborn lambs.

Mallard duck

Rabbit

Robin

A robin builds its nest.

To keep her eggs warm, the mallard duck sits on them in a nest made of soft reeds.

This mother rabbit and her two babies are eating.

Duckling

Robin chicks

Late spring

The robin has laid her eggs and they have hatched. Now she is feeding her chicks with worms.

All the baby animals are growing quickly.

The mallard duck has kept her eggs warm and they have hatched. Now she has six ducklings.

15

Swallows have returned from their winter migration.

Summer

Spring soon turns into summer.

In summer, the sun is very high in the sky, which means that there is daylight for much longer.

Butterflies warm themselves in the sun. Then they are able to fly.

Red Admiral butterfly

Caterpillar munching a leaf

Swallow

The robin chicks learn to fly.

Bee

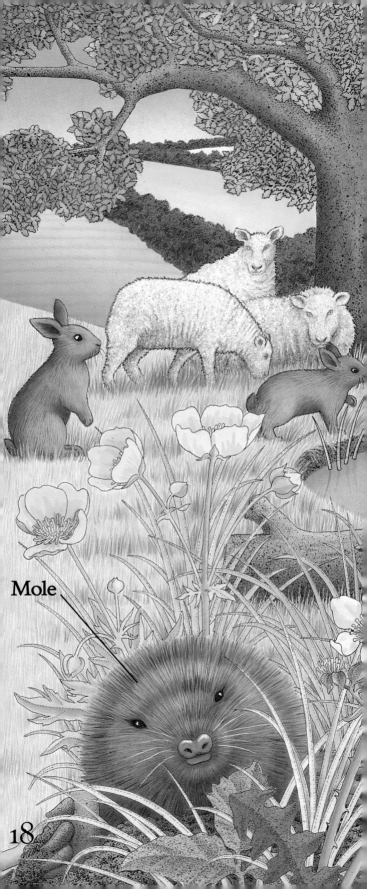

Mole

Late summer

The young lambs,
ducklings and rabbits
are almost fully grown.

The blackberry bush is
now in full flower.

Blackberry
flowers

A mole has come out
of the tunnel he has
been digging.

Ladybird

19

Autumn

As summer changes to autumn, the weather becomes cooler.
The days become shorter.

The oak tree's leaves start to dry out. Their colour changes from green to yellow to a rich red-brown.

The flowers on the blackberry bush slowly turn into red berries.

The male mallard (called a drake) has grown new feathers for winter.

Drake

Berries

Field vole

21

The swallows are getting ready to fly south to a warmer country.

Swallow

Late autumn

Most of the leaves on the oak tree have become a rich, deep brown colour. Soon the wind blows them off the tree.

Field vole

The blackberries are ready to eat. The field vole enjoys them. He needs to eat a lot to fatten up so he can survive through the winter.

23

Winter

As autumn changes to winter, the days become shorter and colder.

The fox is searching hard for food.

The rabbits keep warm in their burrow.

Fox

The field vole is sleeping inside the log.

Robin

The robin keeps
warm by fluffing
up his feathers.

Mid-winter

It is now very cold
and frosty. It may snow.
The stream is covered in ice.

Will the hungry fox
survive the winter?
Let's hope so!

27

The cycle of the seasons

Spring starts when the weather begins to warm up. It is the season of new life. Birds lay their eggs.

Slowly it gets warmer and the days get longer. Eggs hatch and lots of baby animals are born.

Summer is the hottest season. Animals and plants grow quickly.

In autumn, the weather cools down. Berries begin to ripen and leaves turn brown.

As autumn continues, it gets colder. Animals prepare for the cold winter months.

Winter is the coldest season of the year. Some animals hibernate. It becomes difficult to find food.

29

Words about the seasons

Acorns
The fruits of the oak tree. They are smooth oval nuts in a cup-like base.

Autumn
The season when it begins to get colder and animals prepare for the winter.

Buds
Tiny growths which stay on the branches of some trees during the winter, when all the leaves have fallen off. They contain new shoots and leaves which come to life in spring.

Ewe
A female sheep.

Hibernate
When animals spend the winter months sleeping for weeks on end in a nest or shelter. They survive on stored fat from food they eat before hibernating.

Mammal
A warm-blooded animal, usually with a backbone.

Migration
A long journey made by some creatures such as swallows. They leave in the autumn when the weather gets colder and travel to warmer places. They return in spring.

Spring
The season when the weather gets warmer and young animals and plants begin to grow.

Summer
The hottest and driest season of the year.

Winter
The season when it is very cold and the days are short. Many animals hibernate throughout the winter.

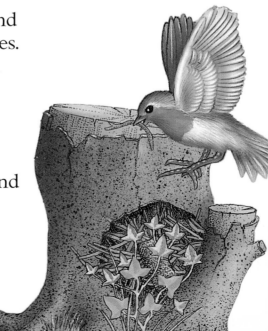

Index

Editors:
Stephanie Cole
Karen Barker Smith

Language Consultant: Natural History Consultant:
Betty Root   Dr Gerald Legg

Created, designed and produced by
The Salariya Book Company Ltd
Book House,
25 Marlborough Place,
Brighton BN1 1UB

Visit the Salariya Book Company at
www.salariya.com

A CIP catalogue record for this book is available from
the British Library.

ISBN 0 7496 4232 7

Published in Great Britain in 2002 by Franklin Watts,
96 Leonard Street, London EC2A 4XD

Franklin Watts Australia
56 O'Riordan Street, Alexandria, NSW 2015

Printed in China.